ChordTime®

Jazz & Blues

>11 Edition

Level 2B

I-IV-V⁷ chords in keys of C, G and F

I-IV-V^7 chords in keys of C, G and F

This book belongs to: _____

Arranged by

Nancy and Randall Faber

Production Coordinator: Jon Ophoff
Design and Illustration: Terpstra Design, San Francisco
Engraving: Dovetree Productions, Inc.

PIANO ADVENTURES®
3042 Creek Drive
Ann Arbor, Michigan 48108

A NOTE TO TEACHERS

ChordTime® Piano Jazz & Blues is a fun-filled collection of jazz standards and appealing blues. The selections motivate students to play while providing valuable practice with rhythm and chords.

As the title *ChordTime®* suggests, the emphasis of this book is on the student's mastery of I, IV, and V⁷ chords. The pieces are arranged in the keys of C, G, and F with valuable warm-up exercises for each key.

ChordTime® Piano Jazz & Blues is part of the *ChordTime® Piano* series. "ChordTime" designates Level 2B of the *PreTime®* to *BigTime® Piano Supplementary Library* arranged by Faber and Faber.

Following are the levels of the supplementary library, which lead from *PreTime®* to *BigTime®*.

PreTime® Piano	(Primer Level)
PlayTime® Piano	(Level 1)
ShowTime® Piano	(Level 2A)
ChordTime® Piano	(Level 2B)
FunTime® Piano	(Level 3A – 3B)
BigTime® Piano	(Level 4)

Each level offers books in a variety of styles, making it possible for the teacher to offer stimulating material for every student. For a complimentary detailed listing, e-mail faber@pianoadventures.com or write us at the mailing address below.

Visit **www.PianoAdventures.com**.

Helpful Hints:

1. Many jazz and blues pieces use *swing rhythm*. Here the quarter note beat is divided into a long and then a short eighth note, rather than being equally divided. It is approximately the same as ♩ ♪. Use this "lilting" of the eighth notes whenever the tempo marking says *swing*.

2. Rhythmic continuity can be improved by having the student tap the piece hands together. (Use the palm or fingertips on the closed fallboard.)

3. Hands-alone practice encourages correct fingering and accurate rhythm.

ISBN 978-1-61677-046-4

TABLE OF CONTENTS

Key of C

Practice these warm-ups before playing the songs in the key of C.

Right Hand Warm-up:

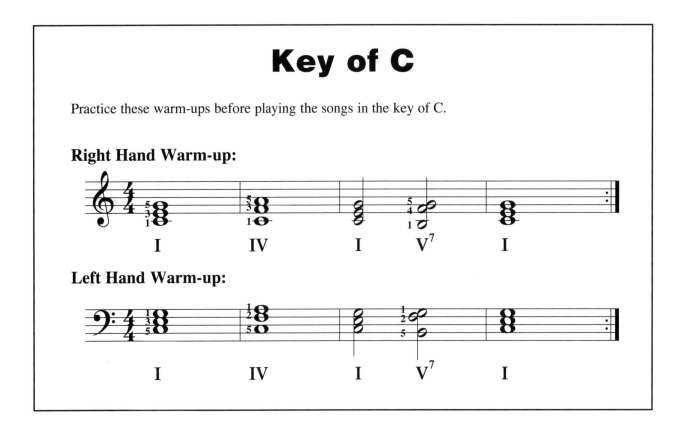

God Bless the Child

Words and Music by
ARTHUR HERZOG JR.
and BILLIE HOLIDAY

Slowly, with feeling

Do Wah Diddy Diddy

Words and Music by
JEFF BARRY and
ELLIE GREENWICH

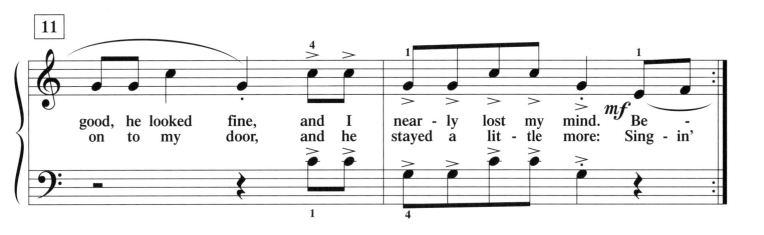

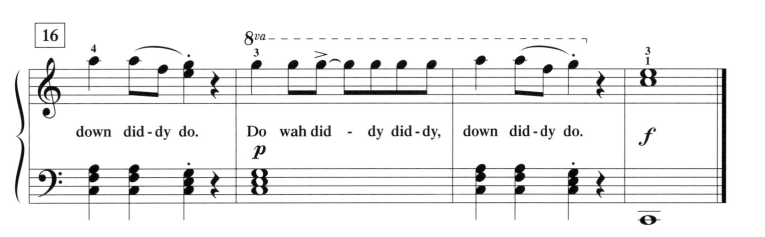

8

Baby Face

Words and Music by
BENNY DAVIS and HARRY AKST

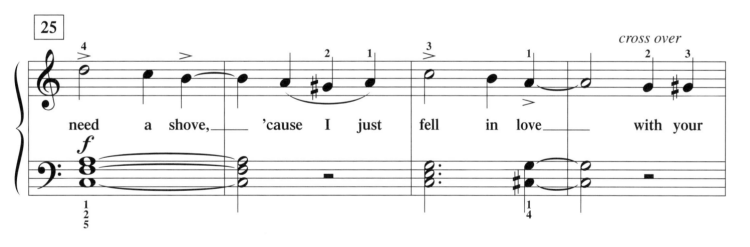

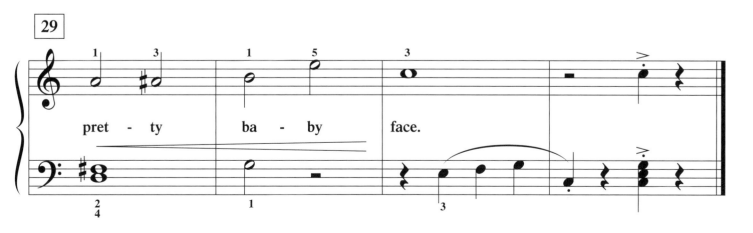

Dill Pickle Stomp

NANCY FABER

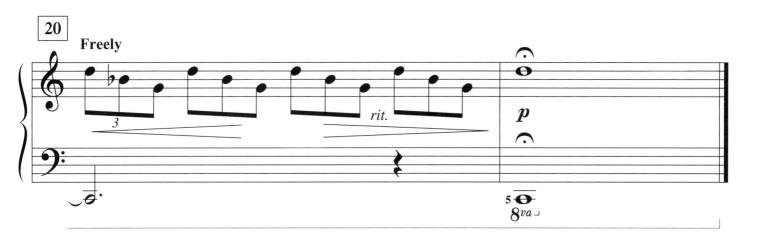

From the Columbia Pictures-Romulus Film *Oliver!*

Where Is Love?

Words and Music by
LIONEL BART

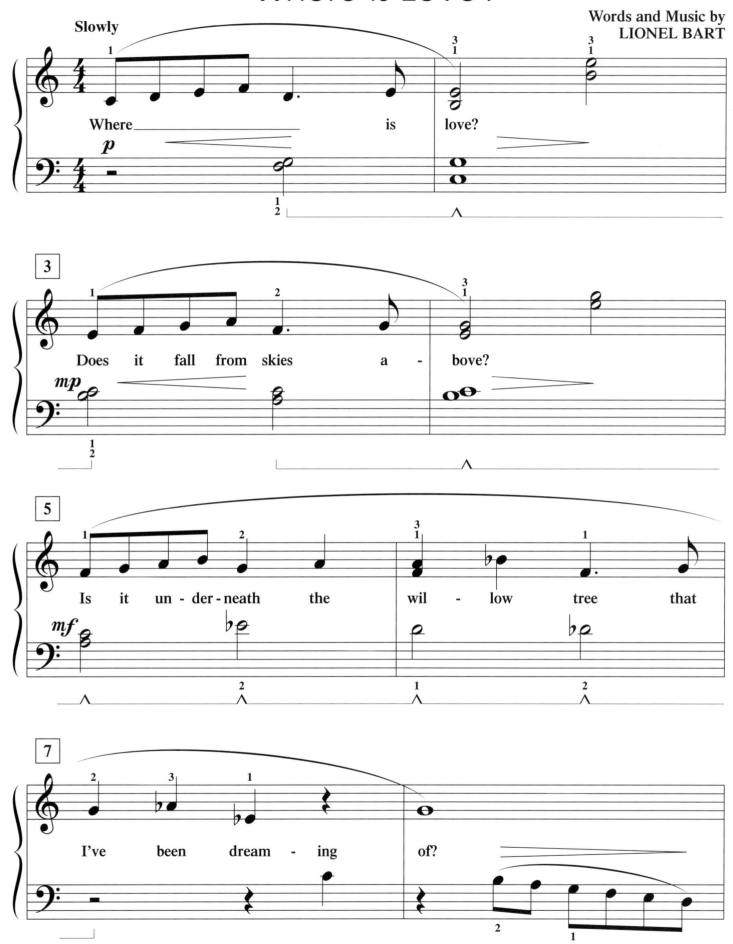

13

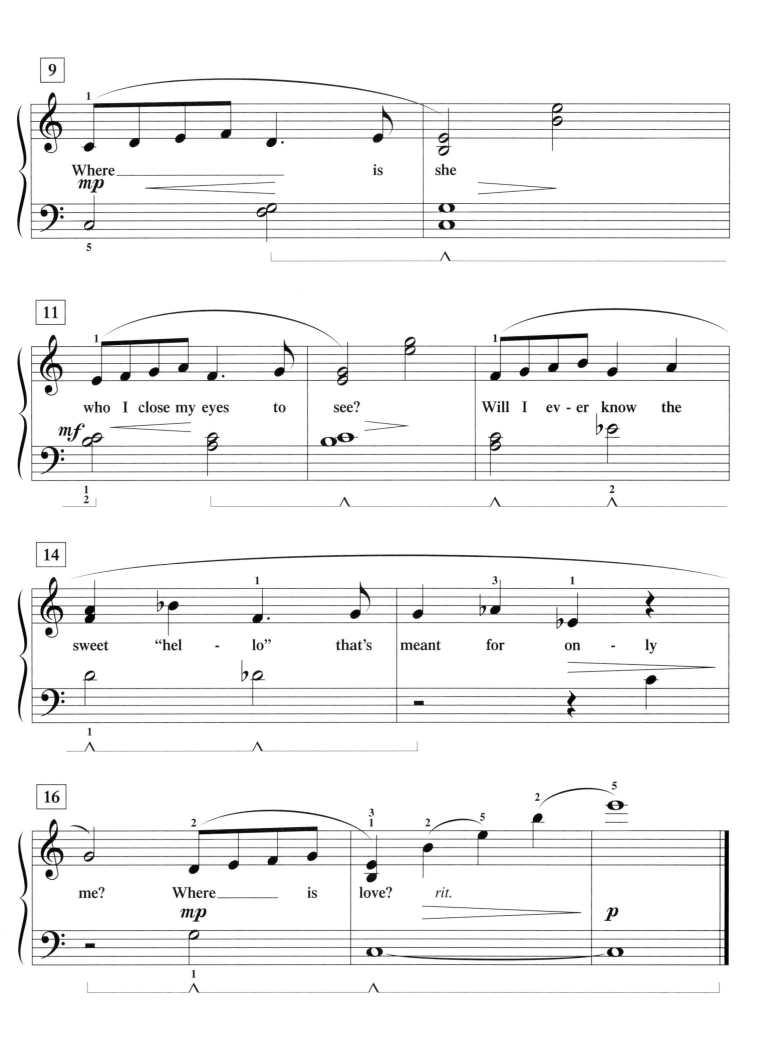

FF1046

Key of G

Practice these warm-ups before playing the songs in the key of G.

Right Hand Warm-up:

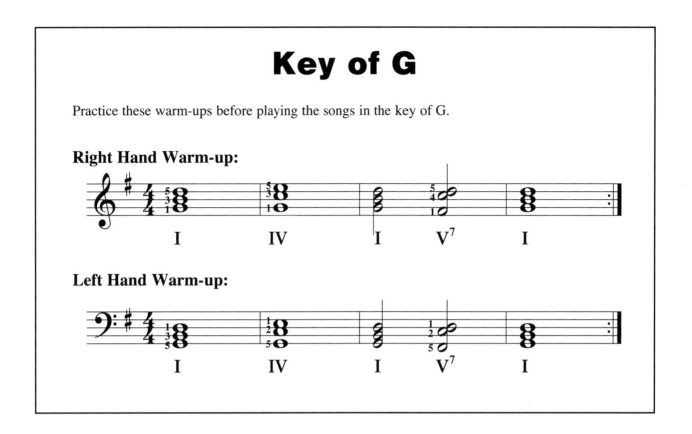

Left Hand Warm-up:

Whistle Stop Blues

Moderately, with a swing (♫ = ♩³♪)

NANCY FABER

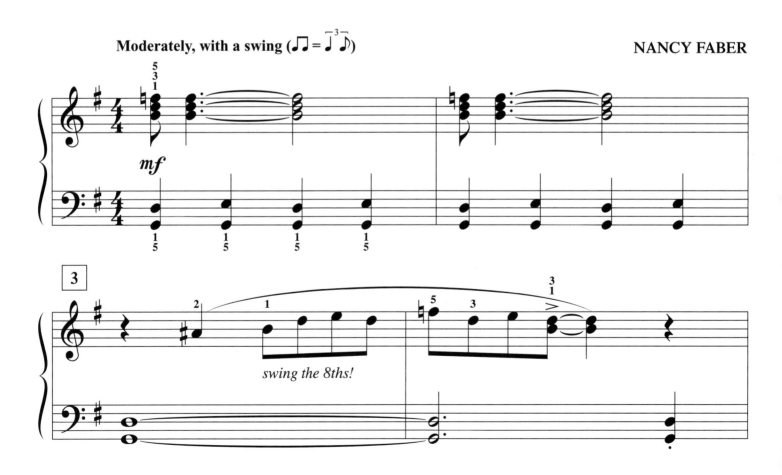

swing the 8ths!

From *Show Boat*
Ol' Man River

Lyrics by OSCAR HAMMERSTEIN II
Music by JEROME KERN

Tuxedo Junction

Words by
BUDDY FEYNE

Music by ERSKINE HAWKINS,
WILLIAM JOHNSON, and JULIAN DASH

With a swing

From *No, No, Nanette*

Tea for Two

Words by
IRVING CAESAR

Music by
VINCENT YOUMANS

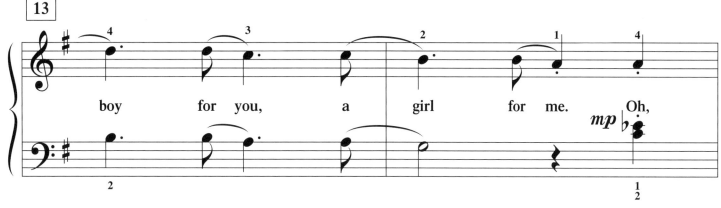

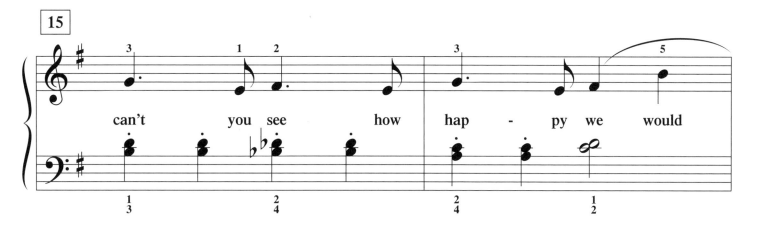

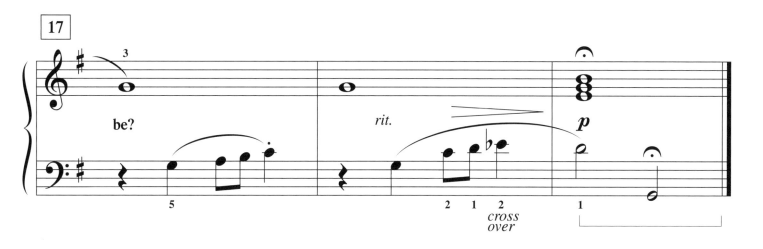

Key of F

Practice these warm-ups before playing the songs in the key of F.

Right Hand Warm-up:

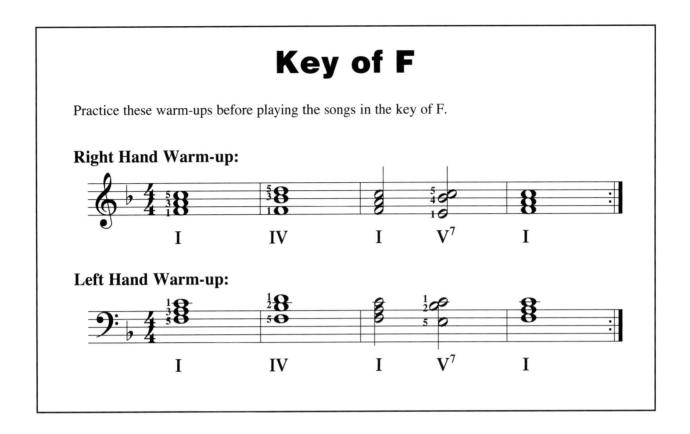

I   IV   I   V⁷   I

Left Hand Warm-up:

I   IV   I   V⁷   I

Left Hand Louisian'

Moderate steady beat

NANCY FABER

FF1046

Watermelon Man

Laid back

By HERBIE HANCOCK

Ain't Misbehavin'

Words by
ANDY RAZAF

Music by
THOMAS "FATS" WALLER
and HARRY BROOKS

When the Saints Go Rockin' In

TRADITIONAL